My First Words: German

AGNIESZKA MURDOCH

www.5minutelanguage.com

ANIMALS

eine Kuh

ein Schaf

ein Vogel

ein Affe

ein Hund

eine Katze

ein Pferd

ein Schwein

ein Tiger

ein Hase

eine Schildkröte

ein Fisch

ein Bär

ein Fuchs

ein Löwe

ein Elefant

FRUIT AND VEGETABLES

eine Orange

eine Kirsche

eine Zitrone

ein Apfel

eine Banane

eine Birne

eine Pflaume

eine Tomate

eine Karotte

eine Gurke

CLOTHES

eine Hose

ein Kleid

ein Rock

ein Hemd

ein T-Shirt

ein Pullover

ein Mantel

eine Jacke

Schuhe

eine Mütze

Handschuhe

ein Schal

Socken

COLOURS

rot

blau

grün

gelb

lila

grau

rosa

braun

orange

schwarz

weiß

NUMBERS

1 eins

2 zwei

3 drei

4 vier

5

fünf

6

sechs

7

sieben

8

acht

9

neun

10

zehn

AT HOME

ein Bild

ein Sofa

ein Bett

ein Stuhl

ein Tisch

ein Fenster

eine Tür

ein Regal

ein Schreibtisch

ein Kleiderschrank

OUTSIDE

ein Baum

eine Blume

eine Straße

ein Haus

TRANSPORT

ein Flugzeug

ein Boot

ein Taxi

ein Auto

ein Bus

ein Zug

ein Fahrrad

ein Laster

ein Hubschrauber

For more information about how to learn
foreign languages effectively, visit:
www.5minutelanguage.com

Printed in Great Britain
by Amazon

63917025R00020